CW00418281

LONG TERM DECISION MAKING

Revision Workbook

Teresa Clarke FMAAT

LONG TERM DECISION MAKING
BY TERESA CLARKE FMAAT

WORKBOOK

Chapter 1 – Introduction

I have written this workbook to assist students who are studying bookkeeping or accountancy. It is not designed as a teaching tool but more of a revision workbook. I hope it will help you to consolidate your studies so that you can become more confident with this topic and enable you to feel more comfortable with those tricky exam questions.

Long term decision making is part of management accounting. This usually focuses on decisions that will last more than 12 months. In this workbook we will be looking at the following and working through some practice questions. We will work through each of these topics in turn and then bring them together in some more complex, exam style practice tasks.

- Payback period
- Net present value
- Net present cost
- Internal rate of return

The <u>payback period</u> is the length of time it takes to "get your money back". I would always recommend using a table to calculate this, even if the task does not require it. It helps to work out the correct answer and avoid errors.

The <u>net present value</u> is the positive or negative benefit of an investment in present value terms. This takes into account the cost of capital which can be interest charges or inflation. Basically £100 today will not be worth the same in 10 years' time, so we use net present value to work out the value in present day terms. We want to see a positive NPV to show that the project will make money. A negative NPV tells us that the project will lose money.

The <u>net present cost</u> uses the cost instead of the revenues to determine the cost of the investment. This also takes into account the cost of capital to work out the cost in present day terms. Exam questions will usually ask you to compare two projects and comment on which one should be recommended. Because this is net present cost, we are looking for the project with the lowest net present cost.

The <u>internal rate of return</u> is the discount rate at which a project achieves a breakeven or the point at which the net present value is zero. Although we will look at how to calculate this, an exam question at Level 3 will more commonly ask you to estimate the IRR in a multiple-choice style question.

<u>Remember</u>: Use a calculator to check all your workings, even if you are good at maths. I will be suggesting methods to work out the payback period, for example, but you can use any method that works for you. There is no wrong method if it gets the correct answer.

Chapter 2 − Tasks with worked answers

Task 1:

If Ricardo buys a machine for a new process for £100,000, it will bring him the following returns.

Year 1:   Net cash inflow   £25,000

Year 2:   Net cash inflow   £30,000

Year 3:   Net cash inflow   £40,000

Year 4:   Net cash inflow   £20,000

What is the payback period for this investment?

In other words, how long will it take or Ricardo to get his money back?

Hint: You might find it helpful to use this table.

Year	Net cashflow £	Cumulative balance £
0	−100,000	−100,000
1	25000	−75,000
2	30 000	−45,000
3	40 000	−5,000.
4	20 000	15,000.

£20,000 =J
£÷1yr : 3mom
3 yr
3 mom

Task 1: worked answer

If Ricardo buys a machine for a new process for £100,000, it will bring him the following returns.

Year 1:   Net cash inflow   £25,000

Year 2:   Net cash inflow   £30,000

Year 3:   Net cash inflow   £40,000

Year 4:   Net cash inflow   £20,000

What is the payback period for this investment?

This type of task is easier to work through as a table:

Year	Net cashflow £	Cumulative balance £
0	(100,000)	(100,000)
1	25,000	(75,000)
2	30,000	(45,000)
3	40,000	(5,000)
4	20,000	15,000

I have entered all the figures provided in the question.

Year 0 is 'today', the first day of the investment. I have entered £100,000 as this is the cost of the machine and the cumulative balance or running total at this point is minus £100,000.

Year 1 is at the end of the first year. I have entered £25,000 as the year's net money in or cashflow. I have added this to the cumulative balance.

I have entered each year after that and added the balance to the cumulative total.

You can see that after the 4 years, we are finally in a positive or making money on top of the initial investment.

We have a payback period of 3 years and some months. Now we must work out exactly how many months into year 4 that the initial money is paid back.

Note: There are various ways of working this out so if you have your own method and it works, please use it. There are no wrong methods if they get to the correct answer.

At the end of year 3 we still had £5,000 to payback of the initial investment.

During year 4 we had a total cashflow of £20,000.

How many months will it take to clear the £5,000?

Amount to clear/total cashflow x 12 = months

£5,000/£20,000 x 12 = 3 months

Or

(£20,000 / 12 months) = 1 month's cashflow.

£1,667 = 1 month's cashflow.

Amount to clear / 1 month's cashflow = months.

£5,000 / £1,667 = 3 months.

Note: You always round up for the number of months as the payback would be at the end of the month.

Answer: 3 years and 3 months.

Task 2:

Francis is considering investing £200,000 into a new manufacturing process. The costs and revenues are given in the table below.

Year	Revenue £	Costs £
1	30,000	10,000
2	50,000	15,000
3	100,000	25,000
4	100,000	25,000
5	80,000	20,000

Using the table below, calculate the payback period for this project.

Year	Revenue £	Costs £	Net cashflow £	Cumulative total £
0				
1				
2				
3				
4				
5				

Note: Revenue – costs = net cashflow. Use net cashflow to calculate the payback period.

Task 2: worked answer

Francis is considering investing £200,000 into a new manufacturing process. The costs and revenues are given in the table below.

Year	Revenue £	Costs £
1	30,000	10,000
2	50,000	15,000
3	100,000	25,000
4	100,000	25,000
5	80,000	20,000

Using the table below, calculate the payback period for this project.

We start by entering the initial investment as a minus figure in the costs column and carrying this over to the net cashflow and cumulative total as there are no other figures at day 1.

At the end of year 1, we have revenue or income of £30,000 and costs or expenses of £10,000, which gives us a net cashflow of £20,000. The £20,000 is added to the cumulative total.

We continue the same process through the whole table. The negative numbers change to positive figures in the cumulative total column as the years progress.

Year	Revenue £	Costs £	Net cashflow £	Cumulative total £
0	0	200,000	(200,000)	(200,000)
1	30,000	10,000	20,000	(180,000)
2	50,000	15,000	35,000	(145,000)
3	100,000	25,000	75,000	(70,000)
4	100,000	25,000	75,000	5,000
5	80,000	20,000	60,000	65,000

The table is complete. We can work out the payback period now from this information. By the end of year 4, we have a positive number which means that the initial investment has been paid back. But we need to work out how many months into year 4 that the initial investment was paid back. Remember to use whatever method you like for this calculation so long as you get the correct answer.

(£75,000 / 12 months) = 1 month's cashflow

£6,250 = 1 month's cashflow

£70,000 / £6,250 = 11.2 months, so actually another whole year.

Answer: 4 years.

Task 3:

Klaudia has asked you to calculate the net present value of a 4-year project as she does not want to tie up cash unless the project is worthwhile. She is aware that inflation reduces the value of money over time and is concerned that her investment may produce a negative value when taking this into consideration. She has provided you with the following figures and asked you to calculate the net present value of the project.

The initial cost of the investment will be £100,000. At the end of the project the machinery involved will have a scrap value of £10,000. The anticipated sales revenues (income) and operating costs (expenses) are given in the table below. The discount factor to be used for the project will be 10%.

Note: The figures for the discount factor percentages will always be given to you in an AAT Level 3 task but if you are studying at a higher level you may have to look them up.

Year	Sales revenue £	Operating costs £
1	80,000	20,000
2	70,000	20,000
3	80,000	30,000
4	50,000	15,000

Discount factor: 10%

Year 0	Year 1	Year 2	Year 3	Year 4
1.000	0.909	0.826	0.751	0.683

Complete the table below to calculate the net present value (NPV) of the project.

	Year 0	Year 1	Year 2	Year 3	Year 4
Capital expenditure					
Scrap value					
Sales revenue					
Operating costs					
Net cashflow					
PV / Discount Factor					
Discounted cashflow					
Net present value					

Task 3: worked answer

Klaudia has asked you to calculate the net present value of a 4-year project as she does not want to tie up cash unless the project is worthwhile. She is aware that inflation reduces the value of money over time and is concerned that her investment may produce a negative value when taking this into consideration. She has provided you with the following figures and asked you to calculate the net present value of the project.

The initial cost of the investment will be £100,000. At the end of the project the machinery involved will have a scrap value of £10,000. The anticipated sales revenues (income) and operating costs (expenses) are given in the table below. The discount factor to be used for the project will be 10%.

Note: The figures for the discount factor percentages will always be given to you in an AAT Level 3 task but if you are studying at a higher level you may have to look them up.

Year	Sales revenue £	Operating costs £
1	80,000	20,000
2	70,000	20,000
3	80,000	30,000
4	50,000	15,000

Discount factor: 10%

Year 0	Year 1	Year 2	Year 3	Year 4
1.000	0.909	0.826	0.751	0.683

Complete the table below to calculate the net present value (NPV) of the project.

We take all the information from the question now and put it into the table. Remember that Year 0 is day 1 and this is the initial investment. Remember that the scrap value is at the end of the project, so is income in year 4. Money in is a positive number. Money out is a negative number. Work out the net cashflow for each year and multiply this by the discount factor to calculate the discounted cashflow.

£	Year 0	Year 1	Year 2	Year 3	Year 4
Capital expenditure	(100,000)	0	0	0	0
Scrap value	0	0	0	0	10,000
Sales revenue	0	80,000	70,000	80,000	50,000
Operating costs	0	(20,000)	(20,000)	(30,000)	(15,000)
Net cashflow	(100,000)	60,000 *80,000 – 20,000*	50,000 *70,000 – 20,000*	50,000 *80,000 – 30,000*	45,000 *10,000 + 50,000 –15,000*
PV / Discount Factor	1.000	0.909	0.826	0.751	0.683
Discounted cashflow	(100,000) *100,000 x 1.000*	54,540 *60,000 x 0.909*	41,300 *50,000 x 0.826*	37,550 *50,000 x 0.751*	30,735 *45,000 x 0.683*
Net present value	64,125 *Total of all discounted cashflows*				

Each year is totalled downwards and then the discounted cashflows are all added together.

The answer is £64,125 and this is a positive number. This means that the project is worth investing even when the time value of money is taken into consideration.

If you are asked to comment on the viability of a project this is the most important factor. If it is a positive number, there is money to be made. If it is a negative number, there is a potential loss to be made.

Take a moment to read through the workings to ensure that you understand the calculations before moving on.

Task 4:

Charlotte is considering replacing a large piece of machinery on her production line. She has provided you with the following information about the capital expenditure and running costs of two different machines. Both will have the same lifespan of 3 years but with different purchase costs and operating costs, and no scrap value at the end with either machine. She would like you to calculate the net present cost of each machine after the 3 years to establish which one has the lower cost. Charlotte has asked you to use a discount factor (or PV factor) of 15% for these calculations.

Note: When we are calculating the net present cost, we are looking for the lowest cost, rather than the highest value as we were with NPV.

Machine A	Year 0	Year 1	Year 2	Year 3
Capital investment £	500,000			
Operating costs £		200,000	250,000	280,000

Machine B	Year 0	Year 1	Year 2	Year 3
Capital investment £	700,000			
Operating costs £		380,000	180,000	100,000

Use the tables below to calculate the net present cost for each project and comment on the results.

Note: The discount factor percentages have already been entered into the tables. Do not use negative numbers as these are all costs.

Machine A	Year 0	Year 1	Year 2	Year 3
Capital investment £				
Net cashflow (costs) £				
PV Factors 15%	1.000	0.870	0.756	0.658
Discounted cashflow £				
Net present cost £				

Machine B	Year 0	Year 1	Year 2	Year 3
Capital investment £				
Net cashflow (costs) £				
PV Factors 15%	1.000	0.870	0.756	0.658
Discounted cashflow £				
Net present cost £				

Task 4: worked answer

Charlotte is considering replacing a large piece of machinery on her production line. She has provided you with the following information about the capital expenditure and running costs of two different machines. Both will have the same lifespan of 3 years but with different purchase costs and operating costs, and no scrap value at the end on either machine. She would like you to calculate the net present cost of each machine after the 3 years to establish which one has the lower cost. Charlotte has asked you to use a discount factor (or PV factor) of 15% for these calculations.

Note: When we are calculating the net present cost, we are looking for the lowest cost, rather than the highest value as we were with NPV.

Machine A	Year 0	Year 1	Year 2	Year 3
Capital investment £	500,000			
Operating costs £		200,000	250,000	280,000

Machine B	Year 0	Year 1	Year 2	Year 3
Capital investment £	700,000			
Operating costs £		380,000	180,000	100,000

Use the tables below to calculate the net present cost for each project and comment on the results.

Note: The discount factor percentages have already been entered into the tables. Do not use negative numbers as these are all costs.

We enter the information provided in the tables above first.

Then we multiply the net cashflow by the discount factor or PV factor percentage for each year.

We total the discounted cashflows which gives us the net present cost for each machine.

We are looking for the machine with the lowest net present cost.

Machine A	Year 0	Year 1	Year 2	Year 3
Capital investment £	500,000			
Net cashflow (costs) £		200,000	250,000	280,000
PV Factors 15%	1.000	0.870	0.756	0.658
Discounted cashflow £	500,000	174,000	189,000	184,240
Net present cost £	1,047,240			

Machine B	Year 0	Year 1	Year 2	Year 3
Capital investment £	700,000			
Net cashflow (costs) £		380,000	180,000	100,000
PV Factors 15%	1.000	0.870	0.756	0.658
Discounted cashflow £	700,000	330,600	136,080	65,800
Net present cost £	1,232,480			

Machine A as the lower net present cost so this would be the cheaper machine to buy and use.

Task 5:

You have been provided with the NPV for a project using two different discount rates or PV factors. The results are shown below.

NPV using a discount factor of 10% = £4,400

NPV using a discount factor of 20% = -£31,000

Estimate the internal rate of return (IRR) for this project.

Remember: The IRR is the discount factor percentage at which the NPV is zero.

Hint: Use my number line method for this.

Find the difference between the percentages.

Find the difference between the results.

Divide the difference in results by the difference in percentages.

This will give the change in value per percentage.

Divide the lower number by this to estimate how many percent to add to the lower rate.

IF YOU ARE CONFUSED NOW, DON'T WORRY, TAKE A LOOK AT THE WORKED ANSWER!

Task 5: worked answer

You have been provided with the NPV for a project using two different discount rates or PV factors. The results are shown below.

NPV using a discount factor of 10% = £4,400

NPV using a discount factor of 20% = –£31,000

Estimate the internal rate of return (IRR) for this project.

Remember: The IRR is the discount factor percentage at which the NPV is zero.

We can use the number line steps for this task now.

Find the difference between the percentages.

20% – 10% = 10%

Find the difference between the results.

–£31,000 – £4,400 = £35,400   (*watch those negative numbers!*)

Divide the difference in results by the difference in percentages.

£35,400 / 10 = £3,540

This will give the change in value per percentage.

£3,540 = for every 1% increase

Divide the lower number by this to estimate how many percent to add to the lower rate.

£4,400 / £3,540 = 1.24

Now add 1.24 to the percentage associated with the £4,400 answer.

10% + 1.24% = 11.24%

Answer: IRR = 11.24%

It might be a good idea to write out these steps in your own way before tackling another task like this.

Note that most level 3 exam questions will only ask for an estimate of the IRR. If you understand how it is calculated it will make it easier for you to estimate the IRR.

Chapter 3 – Tasks

The answers to these questions are at the back of the workbook.

Task 6:

Julie is considering purchasing a new machine to produce a new product. She has provided you with the following information about the initial capital cost, the sales income, and the operating costs for the proposed process which will end after 3 years.

Initial cost of machine   £620,000

Sales income:

Year 1 - £300,000   Year 2 - £400,000   Year 3 - £500,000

Operating costs:

Year 1 - £80,000   Year 2 - £100,000   Year 3 - £120,000

Julie appraises new projects using a 15% cost of capital. (This is the PV factor or discount factor rate).

1. Complete the table below to calculate the net present value of this proposed new machine.

2. Calculate the payback period.

3. Comment on your results.

	Year 0 £	Year 1 £	Year 2 £	Year 3 £
Initial capital investment				
Sales income/revenue				
Operating costs				
Net cashflow				
Discount factors/PV factors	1.000	0.870	0.756	0.658
Discounted cashflow				
Net present value				

The payback period is ....years and ....months.

Workings:

Comment:

Task 7:

Katarina wants to invest in a new process at her factory. She has provided you with the following information about costs for two possible machines for the process.

Machine R	Year 0 £	Year 1 £	Year 2 £	Year 3 £	Year 4 £
Initial investment	60,000				
Operating costs		11,000	12,000	12,000	11,000

Machine S	Year 0 £	Year 1 £	Year 2 £	Year 3 £	Year 4 £
Initial investment	80,000				
Operating costs		8,000	10,000	10,000	9,000

Katarina appraises her capital investments using a 10% cost of capital. The PV factors for this are shown below:

Year	0	1	2	3	4
PV Factor	1.000	0.909	0.826	0.751	0.683

Complete the tables below to calculate the net present cost for each process and comment on your results.

Machine R	Year 0 £	Year 1 £	Year 2 £	Year 3 £	Year 4 £
Capital investment					
Operating costs					
Net cashflow					
PV Factor					
Discounted cashflow					
Net present cost					

Machine S	Year 0 £	Year 1 £	Year 2 £	Year 3 £	Year 4 £
Capital investment					
Operating costs					
Net cashflow					
PV Factor					
Discounted cashflow					
Net present cost					

Comment:

Task 8:

Complete the following sentences:

The ....is the length of time a new project will take to get the initial investment back.

The ....calculates the value of a new project in present value terms.

When the NPV of a project is a negative number then this should be *accepted/rejected.*

The ....is the discount rate at which the project investment is zero, or the discount rate at which the investment breaks even.

The *net present value/payback period/internal rate of return* is the dominant or most important criteria when appraising an investment.

Task 9:

Reesa is considering purchasing a new machine to make a product for 3 years after which the machine will be sold for scrap. She has provided you with the following information about initial investment, revenue, operating costs and scrap value.

	Year 0 £000	Year 1 £000	Year 2 £000	Year 3 £000
Initial investment	300			
Revenue		150	200	250
Operating costs		70	80	90
Scrap value				50

Use this information to complete the table below to calculate the net present value of this project. Comment on the result.

Note: The cost of capital is 10% and the PV factors have already been entered into the table.

Remember: Income figures are positive numbers and cost figures are negative numbers.

Hint: Don't forget to include the scrap value as an income in the appropriate year.

	Year 0 £000	Year 1 £000	Year 2 £000	Year 3 £000
Capital expenditure				
Revenue				
Operating costs				
Scrap value				
Net cashflow				
PV factors	1.000	0.909	0.826	0.751
Discounted cashflow				
Net present value				

Comment:

Task 10:

Calculate the payback periods for the following investments:

a) Initial investment £3,000

   Net cashflows: Year 1 £1,000, Year 2 £1,500, Year 3 £2,000

Year	Net cashflow	Cumulative total

Workings:

Payback period: ....years and ....months.

b) Initial investment £650,000

Net cashflows:

Year 1:   £300,000

Year 2:   £380,000

Year 3:   £300,000

Year	Net cashflow	Cumulative total

Workings:

Payback period: ....years and ....months.

c) Capital investment £40,000

   Sales revenue:

   Year 1: £12,000   Year 2: £22,000   Year 3: £33,000

Year	Net cashflow	Cumulative total

Workings:

Payback period: ....years and ....months.

Task 11:

The net present value for a new project using a 10% discount factor is: £3,000.

The net present value for the same project using a 20% discount factor is:

–£2,000.

Note: Exam questions will sometimes ask you to estimate the IRR and give you some multiple–choice answers to choose from.

Estimate the IRR (internal rate of return) for this project.

  a) 8%

  b) 16%

  c) 26%

Hint: Use logic to work out which answer is correct if you can. If not, use the method we looked at earlier in the book to calculate the appropriate IRR.

Task 12:

Ulita needs to replace one of her machines in the factory. She has provided you with the following information about the machine she is considering, which is expected to have a useful life of 3 years with a scrap value of £20,000 at the end of that time.

Initial investment   £450,000

Revenue income:

Year 1:   £800,000

Year 2:   £850,000

Year 3:   £900,000

Operating costs:

Year 1:   £600,000

Year 2:   £650,000

Year 3:   £700,000

Ulita appraises new projects using a 15% cost of capital.

1. Complete the table below to calculate the net present value of the proposed new machine.

2. Calculate the payback period for the proposed new machine using the template below.

3. Which of the following is likely to be the IRR for the proposed new machine?

   a) 5% b) 10% c) 17%

Net present value	Year 0 £000	Year 1 £000	Year 2 £000	Year 3 £000
Capital expenditure				
Revenue income				
Operating costs				
Scrap value				
Net cashflow				
PV Factors	1.000	0.8696	0.7561	0.6571
Discounted cashflow				
Net present value				

Payback period

Year	Net cashflow £000	Cumulative total £000

Workings:

Internal rate of return estimate:

Task 13:

LaMontagne Enterprises has appraised two proposed new projects and provided you with the following information.

It is the company policy to accept projects with a positive NPV, with a payback period of less than 3 years and a cost of capital lower than 15%.

Appraisal results:

Project KC	
Net present value	£32,000
Payback period	3 years 2 months
IRR	14%

Project RV	
Net present value	(£11,000)
Payback period	1 year 8 months
IRR	9%

You have been asked to comment on the results and recommend which project should be approved.

Note: Use the information in the table to make your comments and remember the most important criteria.

Comment:

Task 14:

Millward Products have provided you with information regarding the net present cost of two proposed new machines. Millward Products have a policy of rejecting projects with a payback period in excess of 3 years and a cost of capital in excess of 10%.

Machine O	
Net present cost	£13,000
Payback period	2 years 1 month
IRR	8%

Machine M	
Net present cost	£15,000
Payback period	2 years 2 months
IRR	7%

Comment on which machine Millward Products should invest in.

Task 15:

Match the following terms to the correct description:

1. Discounted cashflow
2. Revenue
3. Internal rate of return
4. Payback period
5. Net present value
6. Net present cost

A   The value of a project taking into account the time value of money or cost of capital.

B   Another word for sales income.

C   Cashflow that has been reduced by the cost of capital percentage.

D   The PV factor percentage at which the project will achieve a nil return, or breakeven.

E   The amount of time it takes for the full cost of a project to be recovered.

F   The cost of a project taking into account the time value of money or cost of capital.

Hint: Match the ones you know first and then you will only have one or two left to work out.

LONG TERM DECISION MAKING

Task 16:

Viking Components are considering expanding their product line and looking at the possibility of investing in a new machine.

The new machine will have a useful life of 3 years, after which it will be disposed of with no scrap value.

You have been provided with the following details about the new machine.

	Year 0 £000	Year 1 £000	Year 2 £000	Year 3 £000
Capital expenditure	170			
Sales income		85	80	75
Operating costs		8	10	12

Viking Components appraises new projects using a cost of capital at 15%.

a) Calculate the payback period for the project.

Year	Net cashflow £000	Cumulative total £000

The payback period is ....years and ....months.

b) Complete the table below to find the net present value of the project.

	Year 0 £000	Year 1 £000	Year 2 £000	Year 3 £000
Capital expenditure				
Revenue income				
Operating costs				
Scrap value				
Net cashflow				
PV Factors	1.0000	0.8696	0.7561	0.6575
Discounted cashflow				
Net present value				

c) Complete the following sentence:

The net present value of the project is *positive/negative* and *should/should not* be approved.

Chapter 4 – answers

Task 6:

Julie is considering purchasing a new machine to produce a new product. She has provided you with the following information about the initial capital cost, the sales income, and the operating costs for the proposed process which will end after 3 years.

Initial cost of machine   £620,000

Sales income:

Year 1 – £300,000   Year 2 – £400,000   Year 3 – £500,000

Operating costs:

Year 1 – £80,000   Year 2 – £100,000   Year 3 – £120,000

Julie appraises new projects using a 15% cost of capital. (This is the PV factor or discount factor rate).

1. Complete the table below to calculate the net present value of this proposed new machine.

2. Calculate the payback period.

3. Comment on your results.

We start by entering all the information into the table to calculate the net present value of the proposed new process.

The initial investment is a minus number as this is money going out of the business. The sales income is a positive number as this is income coming in. The operating costs are minus figures as these are costs for the process.

Each year is calculated downwards to work out the net cashflow for each year.

The net cashflow for each year is multiplied by the discount factor (provided) to get the discounted cashflow.

The discounted cashflows are all added together to arrive at the net present value for the proposed project.

	Year 0 £	Year 1 £	Year 2 £	Year 3 £
Initial capital investment	(620,000)			
Sales income/revenue		300,000	400,000	500,000
Operating costs		(80,000)	(100,000)	(120,000)
Net cashflow	(620,000)	220,000	300,000	380,000
Discount factors/PV factors	1.000	0.870	0.756	0.658
Discounted cashflow	(620,000)	191,400	226,800	250,040
Net present value	48,240			

To work out the payback period we need to find out how long it will take for the initial investment to be paid back.

<u>Remember</u>: This is a separate calculation from the NPV and the two are not mixed.

We use the net cashflow each year to work out the running total after each year, or the cumulative balance.

The payback period is 2 years and 4 months.

Workings:

Year 0 (£620,000) Balance (cumulative total) = (£620,000)

Year 1 £220,000 Balance = (£400,000)

Year 2 £300,000 Balance = (£100,000)

Year 3 £380,000 Balance = £280,000

The payback is between year 2 and 3, so 2 years and some months.

Year 3 cashflow £380,000 / 12 months = £31,667 (rounded)

The minus balance at the end of year 2 was £100,000, so how many months net cashflow of £31,667 will it take to clear this, or find the zero point, when all money has been paid back.

£100,000 / £31,667 = 3.16

As we want whole months, it will be after 2 years and 4 months that the money is paid back.

Comment:

> The payback period is 2 years and 4 months which is quite a long time considering that the process will only last for 3 years. The net present value is a positive number which is good. Assuming all other company criteria is satisfied this new investment should be accepted.
>
> <u>Note</u>: Don't worry if your words are nothing like mine. The main points for a comment, are to mention the payback period and to make a point of the fact that the NPV is positive which is good. If the NPV was negative, we would be recommending that the project be rejected.

Task 7:

Katarina wants to invest in a new process at her factory. She has provided you with the following information about costs for two possible machines for the process.

Machine R	Year 0 £	Year 1 £	Year 2 £	Year 3 £	Year 4 f.
Initial investment	60,000				
Operating costs		11,000	12,000	12,000	11,000

Machine S	Year 0 £	Year 1 £	Year 2 £	Year 3 £	Year 4 £
Initial investment	80,000				
Operating costs		8,000	10,000	10,000	9,000

Katarina appraises her capital investments using a 10% cost of capital. The PV factors for this are shown below:

Year	0	1	2	3	4
PV Factor	1.000	0.909	0.826	0.751	0.683

Complete the tables below to calculate the net present cost for each process and comment on your results.

We add all the information from the question into the table. There is no need to use negative numbers in this one as the tables are costs only. Multiply the net cashflow (costs) by the discount factors to arrive at the discounted cashflow. Add these together for the net present cost of each machine.

Machine R	Year 0 £	Year 1 £	Year 2 £	Year 3 £	Year 4 £
Capital investment	60,000				
Operating costs		11,000	12,000	12,000	11,000
Net cashflow	60,000	11,000	12,000	12,000	11,000
PV Factor	1.000	0.909	0.826	0.751	0.683
Discounted cashflow	60,000	9,999	9,912	9,012	7,513
Net present cost	96,436				

Machine S	Year 0 £	Year 1 £	Year 2 £	Year 3 £	Year 4 £
Capital investment	80,000				
Operating costs		8,000	10,000	10,000	9,000
Net cashflow	80,000	8,000	10,000	10,000	9,000
PV Factor	1.000	0.909	0.826	0.751	0.683
Discounted cashflow	80,000	7,272	8,260	7,510	6,147
Net present cost	109,189				

Comment:

The total cost over the lifetime of each machine is given as the net present cost. Taking into consideration the discount factor, we can see that machine R is cheaper to run than machine S. We would recommend that machine R is chosen.

Again, don't worry if your words are a lot different to mine. You just need to recognise that it is the machine with the lower cost that is the best choice.

Task 8:

Complete the following sentences:

The **PAYBACK PERIOD** is the length of time a new project will take to get the initial investment back.

The **NET PRESENT VALUE** calculates the value of a new project in present value terms.

When the NPV of a project is a negative number then this should be accepted/***REJECTED***.

The **INTERNAL RATE OF RETURN** is the discount rate at which the project investment is zero, or the discount rate at which the investment breaks even.

The ***NET PRESENT VALUE***/*payback period/internal rate of return* is the dominant or most important criteria when appraising an investment.

Task 9:

Reesa is considering purchasing a new machine to make a product for 3 years after which the machine will be sold for scrap. She has provided you with the following information about initial investment, revenue, operating costs and scrap value.

	Year 0 £000	Year 1 £000	Year 2 £000	Year 3 £000
Initial investment	300			
Revenue		150	200	250
Operating costs		70	80	90
Scrap value				50

Use this information to complete the table below to calculate the net present value of this project. Comment on the result.

Note: The cost of capital is 10% and the PV factors have already been entered into the table.

Remember: Income figures are positive numbers and cost figures are negative numbers.

	Year 0 £000	Year 1 £000	Year 2 £000	Year 3 £000
Capital expenditure	(300)			
Revenue		150	200	250
Operating costs		(70)	(80)	(90)
Scrap value				50
Net cashflow	(300)	80	120	210
PV factors	1.000	0.909	0.826	0.751
Discounted cashflow	(300)	72.72	99.12	157.71
Net present value	29.55			

Comment:

The net present value is a positive number so the project should be accepted.

Task 10:

Calculate the payback periods for the following investments:

a) Initial investment £3,000

Net cashflows: Year 1 £1,000, Year 2 £1,500, Year 3 £2,000

Year	Net cashflow	Cumulative total
0	(£3,000)	(£3,000)
1	£1,000	(£2,000)
2	£1,500	(£500)
3	£2,000	£1,500

Workings:

The payback is somewhere after 2 years but before the end of 3 years.

Year 3 cashflow / 12 months = 1 month's cashflow.

Year 2 negative balance / 1 month's cashflow = months.

£2,000 / 12 = £167 (rounded)

£500 / £167 = 2.99 = 3 months

Or

500/2,000 x 12 = 3 months

Payback period: **2 years and 3 months**

b) Initial investment £650,000

Net cashflows:

Year 1:   £300,000

Year 2:   £380,000

Year 3:   £300,000

Year	Net cashflow	Cumulative total
0	(£650,000)	(£650,000)
1	£300,000	(£350,000)
2	£380,000	£30,000
3	£300,000	£330,000

Workings:

The point at which the initial investment is paid back is after the end of year 1 but before the end of year 2.

£380,000/12 = 31,667 (rounded)

£350,000 / 31,667 = 11.05, so in this case we need to round up to the full 2 years.

Payback period: **2 years (as we need to round up to the next whole month)**

c) Capital investment £40,000

Sales revenue:

Year 1: £12,000   Year 2: £22,000   Year 3: £33,000

Year	Net cashflow £	Cumulative total £
0	(40,000)	(40,000)
1	12,000	(28,000)
2	22,000	(6,000)
3	33,000	27,000

Workings:

2 years and some months gets us to the point of zero when the money is paid back.

6,000/33,000 x 12 = 2.18, so 3 months

Or whatever method you have found easiest to remember.

Payback period: **2 years and 3 months.**

LONG TERM DECISION MAKING

Task 11:

The net present value for a new project using a 10% discount factor is: £3,000.

The net present value for the same project using a 20% discount factor is:

-£2,000.

Note: Exam questions will sometimes ask you to estimate the IRR and give you some multiple-choice answers to choose from.

Estimate the IRR (internal rate of return) for this project.

a) 8%

b) 16%

c) 26%

We can calculate the IRR as follows:

Difference in the NPV values / difference in the percentages = change in NPV per percentage.

-£2,000 to £3,000 = £5,000

20% - 10% = 10

£5,000 / 10 = £500 per 1%

We need 4 x £500 to clear the -£2,000

Deduct 4% from the 20% to arrive at 16%. This is the IRR.

Using logic:

If discounting a number by 20% gives you -£2,000.

And discounting a number by 10% gives you £3,000.

Then the discount percentage giving you £0 will be somewhere between the two.

As the alternatives were either lower than 10%, higher than 20% or in between the two, the answer will clearly be the 16%.

a) 8% – too low, giving you a higher figure

b) 16% – correct

c) 26% – too high, giving you a lower figure

Task 12:

Ulita needs to replace one of her machines in the factory. She has provided you with the following information about the machine she is considering, which is expected to have a useful life of 3 years with a scrap value of £20,000 at the end of that time.

Initial investment   £450,000

Revenue income:

Year 1:   £800,000

Year 2:   £850,000

Year 3:   £900,000

Operating costs:

Year 1:   £600,000

Year 2:   £650,000

Year 3:   £700,000

Ulita appraises new projects using a 15% cost of capital.

1. Complete the table below to calculate the net present value of the proposed new machine.

2. Calculate the payback period for the proposed new machine using the template below.

3. Which of the following is likely to be the IRR for the proposed new machine?

   a) 5%   b) 10%   c) 17%

Net present value	Year 0 £000	Year 1 £000	Year 2 £000	Year 3 £000
Capital expenditure	(450)			
Revenue income		800	850	900
Operating costs		(600)	(650)	(700)
Scrap value				20
Net cashflow	(450)	200	200	220
PV Factors	1.000	0.8696	0.7561	0.6571
Discounted cashflow	(450)	176.92	151.22	144.562
Net present value	22.702			

Payback period

Year	Net cashflow £000	Cumulative total £000
0	(450)	(450)
1	200	(250)
2	200	(50)
3	220	170

Workings:

50/220 x 12 = 2.73, so 3 months

2 years and 3 months

Or divide the year 3 cashflow by 12 to find one month's cashflow and use that to work out how many months it will take to clear the deficit of £50,000.

Internal rate of return estimate:

Using 15% we have a positive NPV. We would need to discount this more to reduce the positive NPV to zero. So would need to use a higher discount figure or cost of capital.

The most likely IRR from the three choices is:

5%

10%

_17%_

As this is the only one which is higher than the discount factor used in the NPV table.

Task 13:

LaMontagne Enterprises has appraised two proposed new projects and provided you with the following information.

It is the company policy to accept projects with a positive NPV, with a payback period of less than 3 years and a cost of capital lower than 15%.

Appraisal results:

Project KC	
Net present value	£32,000
Payback period	3 years 2 months
IRR	14%

Project RV	
Net present value	(£11,000)
Payback period	1 year 8 months
IRR	9%

You have been asked to comment on the results and recommend which project should be approved.

Note: Use the information in the table to make your comments and remember the most important criteria.

Comment:

Project KC has a positive NPV which is the most important factor. The payback period is slightly more than the company policy, but the IRR is lower than the company's requirements.

Project RV has a negative NPV which is a very important factor. Even though the payback period is well within the company policy and the IRR very low, this project is not viable because the NPV is negative.

Project KC should be chosen over Project RV based on the NPV.

Remember: Your wording will be different to mine, but the most important comment is regarding the NPV. A positive NPV should always be chosen over a negative one. The other factors will follow. If two positive NPVs were given, then we would look for the lower payback period or IRR.

Task 14:

Millward Products have provided you with information regarding the net present cost of two proposed new machines. Millward Products have a policy of rejecting projects with a payback period in excess of 3 years and a cost of capital in excess of 10%.

Machine O	
Net present cost	£13,000
Payback period	2 years 1 month
IRR	8%

Machine M	
Net present cost	£15,000
Payback period	2 years 2 months
IRR	7%

Comment on which machine Millward Products should invest in.

The payback period and IRR are both very similar for both machines and both fall within the requirements of Millward Products. The net present cost of Machine O is £13,000 and the net present cost of Machine M is £15,000. Because we are looking for the lowest <u>cost</u>, I would recommend the purchase of Machine O.

Task 15:

Match the following terms to the correct description:

1. Discounted cashflow – **C**

2. Revenue – **B**

3. Internal rate of return – **D**

4. Payback period – **E**

5. Net present value – **A**

6. Net present cost – **F**

A   *The value of a project taking into account the time value of money or cost of capital.*

B   *Another word for sales income.*

C   *Cashflow that has been reduced by the cost of capital percentage.*

D   *The PV factor percentage at which the project will achieve a nil return, or breakeven.*

E   *The amount of time it takes for the full cost of a project to be recovered.*

F   *The cost of a project taking into account the time value of money or cost of capital.*

Task 16:

Viking Components are considering expanding their product line and looking at the possibility of investing in a new machine.

The new machine will have a useful life of 3 years, after which it will be disposed of with no scrap value.

You have been provided with the following details about the new machine.

	Year 0 £000	Year 1 £000	Year 2 £000	Year 3 £000
Capital expenditure	170			
Sales income		85	80	75
Operating costs		8	10	12

Viking Components appraises new projects using a cost of capital at 15%.

Note: In this answer I have used minus signs instead of brackets. Always check the task details to see how you should present negative figures as both are correct, but the exam might specify one method only.

a) Calculate the payback period for the project.

Year	Net cashflow £000	Cumulative total £000
0	-170	-170
1	77	-93
2	70	-23
3	63	40

The payback period is **2 years and 5 months**.

b) Complete the table below to find the net present value of the project.

	Year 0 £000	Year 1 £000	Year 2 £000	Year 3 £000
Capital expenditure	-170			
Revenue income		85	80	75
Operating costs		-8	-10	-12
Scrap value				0
Net cashflow	-170	77	70	63
PV Factors	1.0000	0.8696	0.7561	0.6575
Discounted cashflow	-170	66.9592	52.927	41.4225
Net present value	-8.6913			

c)   The net present value of the project is *positive*/***negative*** and *should*/***should not*** be approved.

I hope that you have found this workbook useful. If you have any comments you can find me on my Facebook page: Teresa Clarke AAT Tutoring.

Teresa Clarke FMAAT

Printed in Great Britain
by Amazon

69231871R00041